Astronomy Now!™

A Look at URANUS

Suzanne Slade

PowerKiDS press.
New York

To my brother, Fred Buckingham, and his son, Little Freddy

Published in 2008 by The Rosen Publishing Group, Inc.
29 East 21st Street, New York, NY 10010

First Edition

Editor: Amelie von Zumbusch
Book Design: Greg Tucker
Photo Researcher: Nicole Pristash

Photo Credits: Cover, p. 13 (main) © SuperStock, Inc.; p. 5 © AFP/Getty Images; pp. 7 (main), 9 (top), 15 © Shutterstock.com; pp. 7 (inset), 11, 12 (left) Courtesy NASA/JPL-Caltech; p. 9 (main) by Photodisc; pp. 12 (right), 17, 21 (inset) © Getty Images; pp. 13 (inset), 19 Courtesy NASA/JPL; p. 21 (main) © www.istockphoto.com/Lars Lentz.

Library of Congress Cataloging-in-Publication Data

Slade, Suzanne.
    A look at Uranus / Suzanne Slade.
        p. cm. — (Astronomy now!)
    Includes index.
    ISBN-13: 978-1-4042-3831-2 (library binding)
    ISBN-10: 1-4042-3831-X (library binding)
    1. Uranus (Planet)—Juvenile literature. I. Title.
    QB681.S62 2008
    523.47—dc22
                                                    2007009497

Manufactured in the United States of America

Contents

A Far-off Planet

Far off in the dark sky is a beautiful planet named Uranus. You cannot see it with your eyes because it is 1.75 **billion** miles (2.8 billion km) from Earth. To view this greenish blue planet, you need to look through a tool with powerful lenses called a telescope.

If you hopped aboard a spacecraft heading for Uranus, you could not land on the planet. This is because Uranus is made of gas. Just as the gases in Earth's air cannot hold things, the gases that make up Uranus could not hold a spacecraft.

Uranus, seen here, is many times larger than Earth. This huge planet is 31,764 miles (51,118 km) across.

The Seventh Planet

Uranus is the third-largest planet in our **solar system**. This big planet is made mostly of **hydrogen** and **helium** gas. Uranus is known as one of the four gas giant planets, along with Jupiter, Saturn, and Neptune.

Uranus is the seventh planet from the Sun. All the planets in our solar system move around the Sun in paths, called orbits. The amount of time a planet takes to circle the Sun equals one year on that planet. Therefore, it takes Uranus one Uranian year to orbit the Sun once. One Uranian year lasts as long as 84 years on Earth.

Uranus lies between the orbits of the planets Saturn and Neptune. *Inset:* Uranus, seen here, has to travel 10.9 billion miles (17.5 billion km) to orbit the Sun one time!

A Special Spin

As planets orbit the Sun, they also spin. A planet spins around a pretend line through its middle, called an axis. Most planets have an axis that runs from the top to the bottom of the planet. When its axis is in this position, a planet spins sideways, like a top.

However, Uranus's axis goes through its sides. Therefore, the planet spins in a different direction from other planets. Uranus looks like a rolling ball as it spins. Uranus spins around once every 17 hours and 14 minutes. This time is the length of one day on Uranus.

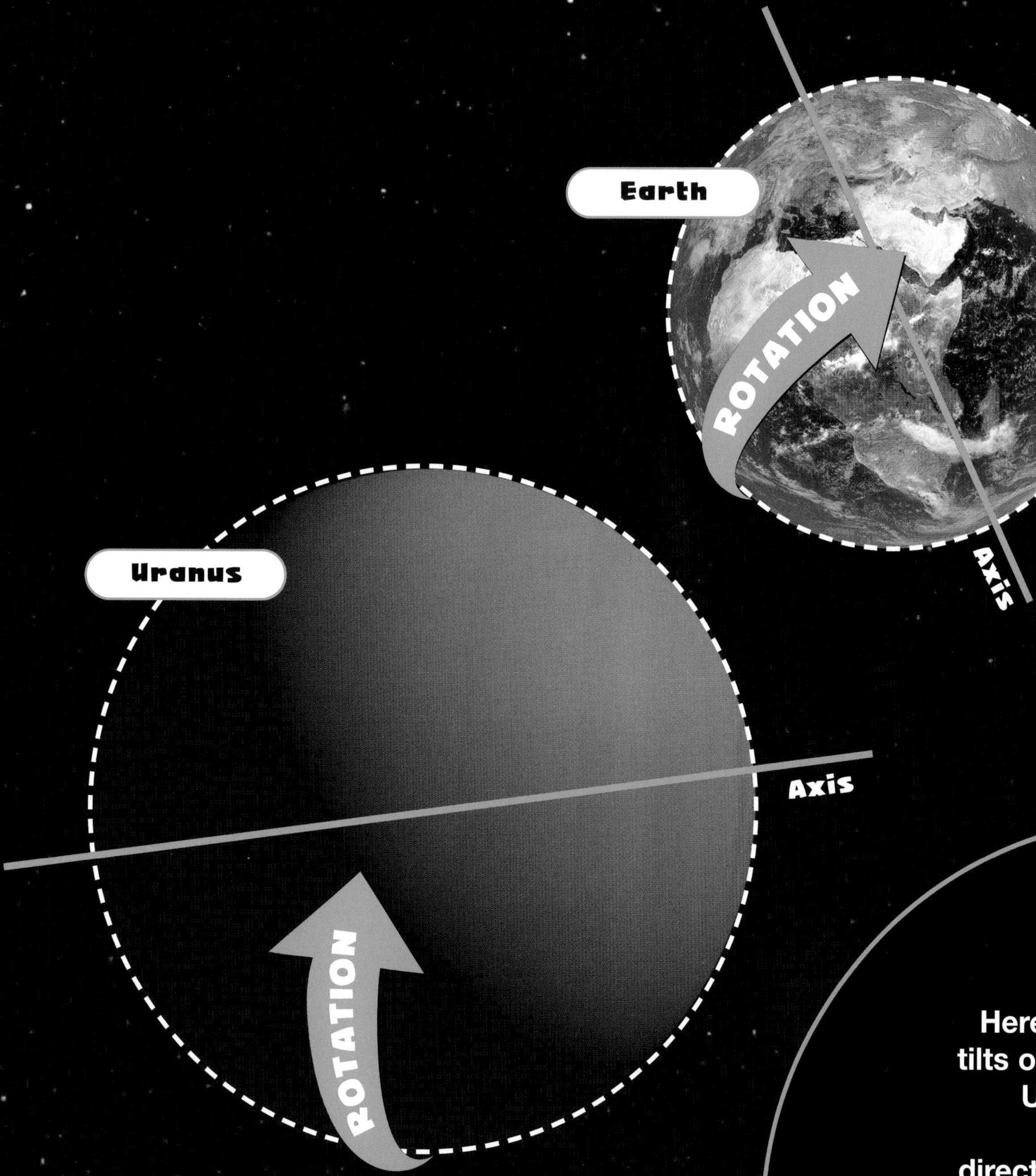

Earth

ROTATION

Axis

Uranus

Axis

ROTATION

Here you can see the tilts of Earth's axis and Uranus's axis. The arrows show the directions in which the two planets rotate, or spin.

9

Big Blue

Uranus is covered by a coat of gases, called an **atmosphere**. These gases include hydrogen, helium, and a small amount of **methane**. The methane blocks certain kinds of light and makes Uranus appear greenish blue. Sunlight is made of many different-colored rays of light. When sunlight hits Uranus, methane takes in the red rays but lets the blue rays through. This results in a bluish planet.

The center part of Uranus is called the core. Most **scientists** think this core is hard and rocky. They believe that melted matter that could be as hot as 9,000° F (4,982° C) circles the core.

Haze, or bits of matter, in Uranus's atmosphere makes the planet look cloudy in this picture. You can see Uranus's blue color underneath, though.

11

Cool Facts

Uranus is home to huge storms and powerful lightning.

Winds can blow as fast as 200 miles per hour (322 km/h) in the atmosphere around Uranus.

Uranus is a very cold planet. It is about -350° F (-212° C) there.

Uranus's Moons

Shakespeare

Uranus's moons are named after characters in plays or poems written by William Shakespeare and Alexander Pope.

The moon Ariel has big holes called craters. It also has many valleys called rift valleys.

Ariel

Uranus's smallest known moon, Mab, was discovered in 2003. This tiny moon is just 6 miles (10 km) wide.

A Uranus Timeline

1977 – The spacecraft *Voyager 2* takes off for Uranus and the other outer planets.

1948 – Gerard Kuiper discovers Uranus's moon Miranda.

1851 – William Lassell discovers Uranus's moons Ariel and Umbriel.

1789 – Herschel discovers Uranus's biggest moons, Oberon and Titania.

1781 – William Herschel discovers Uranus.

Fun Figures

Uranus spins at a rate of about 4 miles per second (6 km/s).

Uranus is about 1.7 billion miles (2.7 billion km) from the Sun.

Each season on Uranus last about 20 years.

Scientists believe Uranus is about 4.5 billion years old.

A Powerful Pull

Some planets have a powerful force called a **magnetic field**. This force can be useful to people. A tool called a compass uses Earth's magnetic field to help people figure out where to go when they get lost.

Earth's magnetic field also causes bands of light called auroras in the sky near the North Pole and the South Pole. Uranus has a magnetic field that causes auroras, too. Earth's magnetic field comes from its core. Scientists believe Uranus's magnetic field is made near the outside of the planet. The pull of Uranus's magnetic field is 48 times stronger than Earth's.

Auroras that form near Earth's North Pole, like the one seen here, are often called the northern lights. Like Earth and Uranus do, the planets Jupiter, Saturn, and Neptune have auroras.

15

Discovering Uranus

Until the late 1700s, people believed that Earth was one of just six planets. Jupiter, Mars, Mercury, Saturn, and Venus were so large and bright that people could spot them easily in the sky. They did not know about Uranus because it was too far away to see.

Then, in 1781, scientist William Herschel found a tiny new disk in the sky. Herschel discovered this disk with a new telescope he had made. This telescope had more powerful lenses than earlier telescopes did. Scientists soon decided this disk was a planet. In time, the planet came to be known as Uranus.

William Herschel, seen here, was a musician who studied the skies in his free time. Over time, he became a well-known scientist. He discovered several moons and studied stars.

Moons Around Uranus

Uranus has at least 27 moons circling it. Scientists hope to find even more moons someday. Uranus's moons are fairly small. Earth's Moon is much bigger than any of Uranus's moons. Uranus's largest moon, Titania, is 980 miles (1,577 km) wide. William Herschel discovered Titania in 1787. Later that year, he spotted Uranus's second-largest moon, Oberon. Oberon is full of deep holes called craters.

Uranus's next three largest moons are Ariel, Umbriel, and Miranda. Of all Uranus's moons, Ariel shines brightest. The darkest moon is Umbriel. Miranda is a very bumpy moon with lots of craters and valleys.

At about 300 miles (483 km) across, Miranda is the smallest of Uranus's five big moons. It is generally as cold as -305° F (-187° C) there.

Uranus's Rings

In 1977, scientists from Australia discovered several rings circling Uranus. Scientists found more rings in 1986, bringing the total number of rings to 11. Uranus's smallest ring is about 1 mile (2 km) wide. The largest may be up to 60 miles (97 km) wide.

Scientists are not certain what these rings are made of. Most scientists believe they are made of dust and large pieces of ice. The ring farthest from Uranus is called Epsilon. It is likely made mostly of ice pieces that are several feet (m) wide. Epsilon is the brightest of Uranus's rings.

Because Uranus spins on its side, the planet's rings circle it from top to bottom. *Inset:* The spacecraft *Voyager 2* took this close-up picture of Uranus's rings.

What's Next?

Voyager 2 is the only spacecraft that has made the long trip to Uranus. After nine years of flying, the spacecraft came within 50,600 miles (81,433 km) of Uranus in 1986. It took pictures that let scientists discover 10 new moons circling Uranus. It also gathered facts about Uranus's magnetic field and atmosphere.

Uranus is so cold that scientists believe nothing can live there, so they are not planning another costly trip to this far-off planet soon. Instead, scientists use the **Hubble Space Telescope** to study Uranus. They hope to find new moons or rings orbiting Uranus without ever leaving Earth!

Glossary

atmosphere (AT-muh-sfeer) The gases around an object in space.

billion (BIL-yun) A thousand millions.

helium (HEE-lee-um) A light, colorless gas.

Hubble Space Telescope (HUH-bul SPAYS TEL-uh-skohp) A tool that was sent into space in April 1990, which has sent back many pictures of Uranus and other planets.

hydrogen (HY-dreh-jen) A colorless gas that burns easily and weighs less than any other known kind of matter.

magnetic field (mag-NEH-tik FEELD) A strong force made by currents that flow through metals and other matter.

methane (MEH-thayn) A gas that burns easily.

scientists (SY-un-tists) People who study the world.

solar system (SOH-ler SIS-tem) A group of planets that circles a star.

Index

Web Sites

Due to the changing nature of Internet links, PowerKids Press has developed an online list of Web sites related to the subject of this book. This site is updated regularly. Please use this link to access the list:
www.powerkidslinks.com/astro/uranus/